FIRST-PERSON STORIES OF THE

GREAT DEPRESSION

BY AVERY ELIZABETH HURT

ROSEN PUBLISHING PRIMARY SOURCE LIBRARY

ROSEN PUBLISHING

Published in 2027 by The Rosen Publishing Group, Inc.
2544 Clinton Street, Buffalo, NY 14224

Designer: Deanna Lepovich
Editor: Nicole Horning

Cataloging-in-Publication Data

Names: Hurt, Avery Elizabeth.
Title: First-person stories of the Great Depression / Avery Elizabeth Hurt.
Description: Buffalo, NY : Rosen Publishing, 2027. | Series: The Rosen Publishing primary source library | Includes glossary and index.
Identifiers: ISBN 9781725342804 (pbk.) | ISBN 9781725342811 (library bound) | ISBN 9781725342828 (ebook)
Subjects: LCSH: Depressions--1929--United States--Juvenile literature. | United States--Economic conditions--1918-1945--Juvenile literature. | New Deal, 1933-1939--Juvenile literature.
Classification: LCC HB3717 1929 H787 2027 | DDC 330.9730916--dc23

Manufactured in the United States of America

CPSIA Compliance Information: Batch #CSRYA27. For further information, contact Rosen Publishing at 1-800-237-9932.

CONTENTS

FOREWORD

History is so much more than just a boring collection of names and dates. It is a collection of stories—sometimes tragic stories, sometimes heroic stories, sometimes romantic stories, sometimes scary stories. And they're all stories of real people who lived real lives.

Those stories can get lost in the shuffle of memorizing battles, studying maps, and listing important court cases or rulers. That's why primary sources are so valuable. They remind us that historical events happened to and because of real people. Reading diaries, looking at photographs, and seeing newspaper articles are just some ways to make history feel personal through primary sources.

Another way is through watching or listening to interviews with people who lived through major historical events. That's what you're invited to do in this book—and all the books that are part of the *Rosen Publishing Primary Source Library*. Each chapter includes quotes from an interview with a real person who experienced a major historical event in a deeply personal way. You can also scan the QR code included at the beginning of each chapter to watch a video interview with the person featured in that chapter.

Created in partnership with Generations Broadcasting, the *Rosen Publishing Primary Source Library* was created to remind readers that there is power in sharing our stories. First-person stories make history come alive. And when history comes alive, we're better able to learn from it—and avoid the mistakes of the past.

The events you're living through today will be part of the next generation's history lessons. As you read and watch the stories collected here, think about what you want your story to be.

Note: More interviews about the topics featured in this series, as well as many other historical events, can be accessed via a subscription to Rosen Publishing's GBC Stories Database: rosendigital.com/GBCStories/.

HOW TO WATCH THE INTERVIEWS FEATURED IN THIS BOOK

- Use your phone's camera, and hold it over the QR code.
- Click the link that appears.
- Watch the video that pops up. If you would like to read a transcript of the interview while you watch, you can click on that option from the menu in the video player.

INTRODUCTION

The Great Depression was the worst economic downturn in United States history. It was catastrophic. Though it started in the United States, it quickly spread to the rest of the world. It lasted more than a decade, from 1929 until around 1941.

In the United States, industrial production dropped by half, banks failed, and many businesses were forced to close. Unemployment was extremely high. Poverty, which was already rampant in many parts of the country, skyrocketed. The **crisis** was especially hard on people of color.

The stock market crash of 1929 is generally said to mark the beginning of the Great Depression. But that wasn't the sole cause of the crisis. The causes were complex, and historians and economists still disagree about some of the details. However, unwise business practices and bad monetary policy were two important factors that contributed to the economic collapse.

The previous decade—known as the Roaring Twenties—had been a time of great prosperity, or so it seemed. But that prosperity was fragile and somewhat of an illusion. Much of it was based on debt, and the distribution of wealth was extremely unequal. After the stock market crashed, the entire house of cards that was the U.S. economy came tumbling down.

Whatever the causes, the consequences were dire. By 1932, one out of every four Americans was out of work. In some cities, eight out of every ten people were unemployed. Many families lost their homes. Some lived in makeshift shelters on empty lots. Hungry people formed lines at soup kitchens hoping to get a meal.

President Herbert Hoover took some steps to help improve the economy. They weren't enough, however. Hoover was a big believer in "rugged individualism" and small government. He did begin some public works programs designed to create jobs, but for the most part, he believed that such programs would be bad for people's character and make them dependent on the government. Hungry, homeless people didn't see it that way. They blamed Hoover for the crisis.

In 1932, Americans elected a new president, Franklin D. Roosevelt. He offered the American people what he called "a

During the Great Depression, hungry people waited in lines that stretched for blocks, hoping for a meal.

New Deal." Roosevelt's New Deal became an extensive network of laws and programs designed to help get the economy back on track and to provide jobs for the unemployed.

The New Deal was a tremendous help, but it did not fix things quickly. The Great Depression did not truly end until the United States entered World War II in 1941. Government investment in the war effort finally revived the economy.

In the following chapters, you are going to meet real people who lived through the Great Depression. These people were children at the time. They discuss what it was like for them and their families. You'll learn about their homes, the games they played, and how they and their families got by during such a hard time.

Hearing from people who were there and learning what it was like for them brings this period of history to life in a more personal way. So read on to learn what life was like for them growing up during the worst economic crisis the United States has ever known.

CHAPTER ONE

SOUP BONES AND CARDBOARD SHOES: GROWING UP IN THE GREAT DEPRESSION

The Great Depression was hard on almost everyone. In some ways, it was hardest on children. Their lives weren't as stable as they would have been in better times, and they had to do without things children living in better economic times take for granted. David grew up in Milwaukee, Wisconsin, during the Depression. Like many people at that time, David and his family faced their share of hardships, but his parents protected their children from the worst of it. In an interview, David shared what those years were like and how his family coped.

WHEN THE BANKS FAILED

One of the most frightening parts of the Great Depression was what happened to the banks. In October 1929, the stock market crashed, then in 1930, many banks began to fail. When a bank failed, it closed its doors and people could lose all the money they had saved there, which was one of the main contributing factors to the Great Depression.

As news spread that the banks were in trouble, people rushed to take out their money, which was called a "bank run." However, banks didn't keep enough cash on hand for everyone to withdraw their savings at once. When too

Scan this QR code to watch David talk about what it was like to be a boy during the Great Depression.

When the banks were failing, people started scrambling to get their money out. A bank run is shown here.

many people showed up, the bank would run out of money and shut down.

For many families, this meant losing everything they had worked for. Money that was meant for food, rent, or the future was suddenly gone. Without that money, it became even harder to survive an already difficult situation.

FAST FACT

DURING THE PEAK OF THE GREAT DEPRESSION, A QUARTER OF THE WORKFORCE WAS UNEMPLOYED. THAT WAS ALMOST 13 MILLION PEOPLE.

To help stop this problem, the government later created new rules to protect people's savings. But during the early years of the Depression, there was no such protection.

The failure of the banks was terrifying to many people. A group of people are shown here with protest signs outside a bank after it failed.

NO SAFETY NETS

Today, many people rely on government programs to help them during hard times. But when the Great Depression began, those programs did not exist. There wasn't unemployment insurance (a program that pays people a part of their wages when they lose their job), no Social Security (a system that provides benefits to the elderly, unemployment insurance, and aid for vulnerable groups such as those with disabilities), and very little federal aid.

If someone lost their job, they had to rely on their savings, family members, or local charities. With banks shutting down and many people's family members in the same hard financial situation, it was very difficult to find any kind of support. Charities didn't have enough resources to support everyone.

This lack of a "safety net" made the effects of the Great Depression much worse. Families who may have been able to recover from a short period without work instead were falling deeper into poverty.

RESOURCEFUL PEOPLE

"It was a tough about four years, five years," David recalled in his interview. Food was hard to come by, but his mother knew how to make do with very little. "My mother went to the butcher shops, and you got soup bones, and you didn't have to pay for them." Soup bones don't sound like much of a meal, but this was often all David's family, and many other families, could afford. "You scraped what meat you could off of there for the **protein**."

David's dad was resourceful too. He didn't scrape the meat off soup bones, but he did know how to make use of other kinds of scraps—things that in better times would be thrown in the trash. "People today wouldn't believe that when you found a piece of cardboard on the road, you took it home so that your dad could make a insole for your shoes." But that's just the kind of thing people had to do when they couldn't afford shoes.

Because there weren't any government relief programs, many people relied on food lines in urban centers such as this one.

Soup kitchens such as this were important during the Great Depression.

FAST FACT

WHEN PEOPLE COULDN'T AFFORD FOOD, CITIES OFTEN LET THEM PLANT "THRIFT" GARDENS ON VACANT LOTS. BETWEEN 1931 AND 1932, DETROIT'S THRIFT GARDEN PROGRAM FED ABOUT 20,000 PEOPLE.

"THE WORST EXPERIENCE"

Finding food and clothing weren't the only challenges David's family faced. They also lost their home. David described this as "the worst experience I could imagine at that age." Still, his family was luckier than many other people who lost their homes during the Great Depression. David's dad was a barber, so the family was able to move into the barbershop.

With a little resourcefulness, David's family made life in the barbershop as homey and comfortable as possible: "[My parents] strung wires and hung sheets that we had [to make] a bedroom for my brother, sisters, and myself. My mother had a kitchen. The folks had a little bedroom for themselves."

David and his family lived in this makeshift home in the back of the barbershop for about a year before David's parents "got back on their feet," as David put it, and were able to move back into a home of their own.

FAST FACT

WHEN PEOPLE COULD NO LONGER AFFORD CERTAIN ACTIVITIES OUTSIDE THE HOME, THEY PLAYED CARDS AND BOARD GAMES AT HOME AND WITH NEIGHBORS. BOTH *SCRABBLE* AND *MONOPOLY* WERE INTRODUCED DURING THE 1930S.

A LOVING MOM

David knew things were tough, but he also said that in some ways he wasn't aware of the massive economic crisis he was living through. There was so much hardship going

Herbert Hoover was president of the United States from 1929 to 1933. His halfhearted response to the Great Depression was a key reason he was defeated by Franklin D. Roosevelt in the 1932 presidential election.

HOOVERVILLES

Many people who lost their homes during the Great Depression weren't lucky enough to have a barbershop to stay in. They had nowhere to go. Often, people without housing would create makeshift camps where they built shelters out of salvaged pieces of wood and tin, and if nothing sturdier was available, of cardboard. These shelters generally had dirt floors and offered little protection from the cold and rain. Of course, in these "towns," clean water and toilets were scarce. Medical care was lacking too.

These camps sprang up in vacant lots, under bridges, and in **culverts** in cities and towns across the United States. These impromptu towns were called "Hoovervilles" in a sarcastic nod to President

Sometimes called "shantytowns," Hoovervilles were a symbol of people's desperation but also their ingenuity and community.

on around him that it seemed just like regular life, he said. When he was asked why the enormity of the situation didn't sink in, he said that was probably because of his mother. "My mother was a very loving woman. I know she protected us in a lot of ways."

To bring in more money for the family, David's mom found a job in a restaurant. In those days, when jobs were so scarce, people

Herbert Hoover. Many people blamed Hoover both for the Depression itself and for refusing to provide direct relief to suffering citizens.

The Hooverville in Seattle, Washington, is one of the best documented of these camps. It spread over 9 acres (3.6 ha) and lasted from 1931 to 1941. At one point, at least 1,200 people lived there, and it had its own mayor.

Hoovervilles weren't the only things named after President Hoover. Newspapers that were used to keep warm were called "Hoover blankets." "Hoover flags" were empty pockets turned inside out.

Despite the sarcastic name and the dire conditions, Hoovervilles were an example of how people came together to help each other survive one of the most challenging periods in the history of the nation.

Hoovervilles acted as their own towns sometimes. A U.S. Mail sign from the Seattle Hooverville is shown here.

took whatever jobs they could find, generally for much lower wages than they would have made at the same job before the Depression hit. David's mom worked the night shift. "She would go to work at 10:00 in the evening, work all night, and come back at 7:00 in the morning to get us off to school and my dad off to work. And then she went to bed, and was still up to make dinner for us."

This photograph of a struggling mother and her children is one of the most famous images to come out of the Great Depression.

As David's story shows, childhood during the Great Depression could be hard. But when families took care of each other, they were able to hang on until times were better.

HOW YOU SEE HISTORY

1. Why do you think David was in some way unaware of the larger crisis he was living through?
2. Many people blamed President Hoover for how they were living. What do you think he should have done to help people during the Depression?
3. Why do you think losing his home was the worst thing David could imagine as a child?

CHAPTER TWO

SOME WERE HIT HARDER THAN OTHERS

Like David, Glenn was a child during the Great Depression. But his experiences were quite different from David's. David was born in 1922, so he was seven years old when the Depression began. Glenn was born in 1934, so by the time he was seven, the Depression was technically over, though many people were still struggling. In his interview, Glenn discussed what it was like for his family during the Depression.

SIMPLER TIMES

The Great Depression was a difficult time for most people, but it was harder for some than for others. For Glenn, growing up in Berwyn, Illinois, a suburb of Chicago, the Depression was not as impactful as it was for families like David's. "Generally speaking," Glenn said, "I had a very pleasant childhood. The Depression made no difference to me whatsoever."

Glenn said that the hard economic times affected his brother, who was four years older, a little more. Still, Glenn had to do without some things, like new clothes. "I had a lot of hand-me-down clothes from my brother because he was four years older."

Having to miss the latest fashion trends wasn't what bothered

Scan this QR code to watch Glenn discuss his family's experience during the Great Depression.

People did what they could to survive and help others during the Depression. This place offered free soup, coffee, and doughnuts for people who were unemployed.

Glenn most. "I never owned a bicycle, a new bicycle," he said. "That's the kind of stuff that affected me as a little kid."

But bicycle or no, Glenn and his friends had a lot of fun during those years. "We played **sandlot ball**. We ice skated." During the winter, the city would flood an area of a local park to create a place for kids to skate. They played "kick the can" and other outdoor games. There were fewer cars, so kids could play games in the street. Hopscotch and marbles were also common games back then. Skipping rope and playing hide-and-seek were popular too.

Kids also read a lot in those days. Some children's books that were popular during the Great Depression were the *Little House* series by Laura Ingalls Wilder, the *Winnie the Pooh* books, and adventure books like *Call of the Wild* by Jack London.

Books written by Laura Ingalls Wilder, such as this one, were a popular choice during the Great Depression.

Glenn said he and his friends did "all these things that normal kids do—I mean, not today. Normal kids I don't think do these kinds of things today," he added. "They're more into electronic stuff and communication."

THE GOLDEN AGE OF RADIO

Even though it was invented in the 1920s, television wasn't common until the 1950s. During the Depression, many families had radios and enjoyed listening to popular radio programs. The 1930s and 1940s are considered the "golden

Impromptu games of sandlot baseball would attract kids and adults from all over town. It was called "sandlot" ball because it was played anywhere you could find a place to play, generally an empty, sandy lot.

Whether it was bringing news or entertainment, the family radio was an essential part of the lives of most Americans during the Great Depression.

FAST FACT

IN 1930, 12 MILLION AMERICAN HOUSEHOLDS OWNED A RADIO. BY 1939, THIS HAD MORE THAN DOUBLED, WITH 28 MILLION HOUSEHOLDS HAVING A RADIO.

age" of radio. Shows broadcast on the radio included westerns, detective programs, **soap operas**, comedies, variety shows, and much more. Gathering around the radio in the evening was a way families like Glenn's could get away from their troubles for a little while. Radio was also the way many families got their news, so it was important to have a radio if you could afford it. Some families were willing to lose the family car if it meant being able to keep their radio.

FIRESIDE CHATS

During the Great Depression, nearly every American felt uncertain and afraid about the future. To help calm and reassure Americans, President Franklin D. Roosevelt used the radio to speak directly to them in a series of talks known as "fireside chats."

In these broadcasts, Roosevelt explained what the government was doing to improve the economy. He spoke in a calm and reassuring way that helped people feel more hopeful. Families would gather around the radio to listen, feeling as if the president was speaking directly to them in their own homes.

Franklin D. Roosevelt is shown here delivering one of his fireside chats.

Shown here is a quote from President Roosevelt, displayed at a memorial dedicated to him in Washington, D.C.

Roosevelt was elected in 1932, started his presidency in 1933, and immediately began taking dramatic steps to end the Depression. Between 1933 and 1944, he delivered 31 fireside chats, using the chats to explain what was happening with the banking crisis, to encourage reopening of the banks, and to drive support for New Deal programs and war efforts.

The chats had an immense impact. Americans felt like the president was speaking directly to them in their living rooms because his chats started with "My friends." Additionally, his encouragement of the banks reopening and explanation of what was happening helped restore public confidence. These chats also helped solidify the perception of Roosevelt as a confident leader during nationwide crises.

FACTORIES SLOW DOWN

The Great Depression affected nearly every industry in the United States. When people stopped buying goods, factories no longer needed to produce as much. As a result, many businesses reduced workers' hours, cut wages, or shut down completely.

Industries that made cars, appliances, and building materials were hit especially hard. Because fewer homes were being built and fewer products were being purchased, the demand for materials like steel

Bookmobiles were popular in the 1930s. When the bookmobile came around, people would come out to choose a few books to read, then turn them back in the next time the bookmobile came to town.

dropped sharply. Even skilled workers could find themselves without work when entire industries slowed down.

> **FAST FACT**
>
> IN 1939, 92 PERCENT OF PEOPLE IN URBAN AREAS OF THE UNITED STATES HAD ACCESS TO PUBLIC LIBRARIES. ONLY 26 PERCENT OF RURAL PEOPLE DID.

PAINTING THE FOUNDRY

Glenn credits his parents for making sure he was able to still enjoy life even when the economy made things hard. He said, "My mother and father did a very good job in those years in raising us, keeping a roof over our heads, keeping food on the table." Though Glenn had to do without new clothes, his parents made sure he and his brother had good shoes, he added.

Glenn's dad was a metallurgist at National Malleable and Steel Casings, a steel foundry in Berwyn. A metallurgist is someone who

WORKS PROGRESS ADMINISTRATION

When private industry couldn't provide enough jobs for people who needed them, the U.S. government stepped in to help. After defeating President Herbert Hoover in the 1932 presidential election, Franklin D. Roosevelt set about creating programs that would bring relief to the people suffering the effects of the Great Depression. One of the most famous of these programs was the Works Progress Administration, or WPA. The WPA, created in 1935, put people to work building bridges, roads, public buildings, parks, and airports.

Harry Hopkins, the man in charge of the program, believed that providing jobs, rather than just payments, was a better way to help people. He believed that if a person was given a **dole**, their body was saved but their spirit, or pride, was destroyed. However, if the person was given a job with steady wages, both their body and spirit would be saved.

Harry Hopkins was the key architect of the Works Progress Administration, a program that kept millions of people out of poverty during the Depression.

FAST FACT

THE WPA EMPLOYED MORE THAN 8.5 MILLION PEOPLE. THEY MADE AN AVERAGE SALARY OF $41.57 A MONTH, WHICH WOULD BE ALMOST $1,000 TODAY. THAT'S NOT MUCH MONEY, BUT IN THOSE DAYS, IT WAS ENOUGH TO EAT AND AFFORD A PLACE TO LIVE.

works with metals. "He made a very decent living doing that," Glenn recalled. "He had a very good job there."

Of course, when the Great Depression hit,

The program also paid women the same amount of money as men for the same work. However, women in the program were more likely to be assigned to lower paying jobs, such as sewing, caring for the elderly, and teaching in nursery schools.

Hopkins, who was a social worker before coming to government service, believed very strongly in preserving people's **dignity**. It was important to him that people felt useful and valued. And the WPA provided that. The work they did helped rebuild the nation's infrastructure. But not all WPA projects were merely practical. Some lifted the spirit too. Artists were paid to create **murals** and sculptures for public buildings; writers were paid to document the historic period. When someone questioned the inclusion of artists in the program, Hopkins would tell them that artists had to eat just like everyone else.

Members of the WPA are shown here building a stairway.

there was very little work for anyone, even people with valuable skills, like Glenn's dad. The steel industry was hit particularly hard because many of the industries that used steel were cutting production. People couldn't afford to buy automobiles, so car manufacturers weren't

FAST FACT

LAGUARDIA AIRPORT IN NEW YORK AND CAMP DAVID IN MARYLAND, WHICH IS A PRESIDENTIAL **RETREAT**, WERE BUILT BY PEOPLE WORKING FOR THE WORKS PROGRESS ADMINISTRATION.

This worker in Pennsylvania is forging steel to make wheels for trains. Much of this kind of work was lost during the Great Depression.

FAST FACT

THE GREAT DEPRESSION REDUCED THE COUNTRY'S STEEL PRODUCTION BY 75 PERCENT. EVEN WORKERS WHO KEPT THEIR JOBS WERE FORCED TO ENDURE WAGE CUTS AND REDUCED HOURS.

producing as many. The construction industry and the household appliance industry, which also used a lot of steel, were in trouble, too. This meant many steel companies went into **bankruptcy** or had to temporarily shut down.

Glenn's dad was lucky. Despite the crisis in the industry, he managed to stay on at the foundry. "He ended up painting the inside of the foundry. Just to keep him, they would keep him employed," Glenn said. "They didn't want to lose him. He was evidently a valued employee." But companies couldn't pay all their employees to paint their factories. With so many people out of work, even low-paying jobs were hard to come by. His dad's position at work was another reason the Great Depression didn't make much of an impression on Glenn as it did on others who lived through it.

HOW YOU SEE HISTORY

1. Unlike David in Chapter One, Glenn said the Depression didn't have much effect on him. Can you think of some reasons for this? How were their lives different?
2. Harry Hopkins thought that it was very important to help preserve the dignity of people who had lost their jobs. Why do you think he felt this way? Do you agree?
3. Imagine you were 8 or 10 years old during the Great Depression. How do you think it would affect you and your family?

CHAPTER THREE

HELPING EACH OTHER

During the Great Depression, life was hard everywhere. But there were some advantages to life in rural America. That's because in many cases, people living in rural areas could grow their own food. Even though there was still not much to eat, they generally had enough to share with others who were hungry. In an interview, Emma Jean recalled how her family, living in a small town in Arkansas, got by and how they helped others during these difficult years.

"WE ATE WHAT WAS AVAILABLE"

Like many adults during the Great Depression, Emma Jean's parents didn't talk much to their children about the hardships they were going through. But the kids noticed, even if they didn't fully understand why times were tough.

"I remember when we were children playing in the snow, we needed to have heavier coats and heavier shoes. I can remember one time we put pieces of cardboard inside the shoes because the soles were so thin, and you'd wear double socks, things that that," Emma Jean recalled. "So I'm sure the money was pretty scarce in our family, but Daddy had a job. A lot of dads didn't have a job." Of course, in those days, even those lucky enough to have a job rarely

Scan this QR code to watch Emma Jean talk about what it was like growing up in rural America during the Great Depression.

This sculpture depicts men lining up during the Great Depression. Lines of men in suits and hats waiting for food was common during this time.

made good enough wages to live comfortably.

Another thing that protected Emma Jean and her brothers and sisters, at least from the severe hunger many people faced, was the family's vegetable garden. "Dad and Mother would work in the garden out behind the house," she said.

FAST FACT

THOUGH BACKYARD GARDENS PROVIDED FOOD FOR MANY FAMILIES, FARMERS WERE HIT HARD BY THE GREAT DEPRESSION. BY 1933, ABOUT ONE-THIRD OF FARMERS HAD LOST THEIR LAND.

Emma Jean's family grew corn, potatoes, onions, radishes, "all those spring things," she recalled. "If we didn't have the right, or enough of, food to eat, we didn't know it," she said. "We ate what was available." Having a garden meant they could help other hungry people too.

DUST STORMS AND DROUGHTS

While families across the country were struggling with the economy and having enough food to eat, people living on the Great Plains faced additional disasters. This region, which included Oklahoma, Texas, and Kansas, experienced a long period of drought. With little rain to hold the soil in place, strong winds picked up dry dirt and carried it through the air in massive dust storms. This earned the area the name "the Dust Bowl."

Dust storms filled the air in the Great Plains, causing people to move away and search for homes and jobs elsewhere. This man is caught in a thick dust storm.

These storms could darken the sky in the middle of the day. Dust covered homes, filled the air people breathed, and ruined crops. Farmers who had once been able to grow enough food to support their families suddenly found their land turning to dust.

Many families were forced to leave their homes and travel west in search of work. These families were sometimes called "Okies," even if they weren't from Oklahoma. They often packed everything they owned into cars or trucks and headed to places like California, hoping to find jobs picking fruits and vegetables.

Moving was incredibly difficult. Children often had to leave school, and parents had to make decisions about where to go next. Jobs were hard to find, and many lived in crowded camps with little food or clean water. Still, they kept moving forward, hoping to build a better life.

Migrant families stayed in small tents with whatever necessary belongings they could take with them.

Signs such as these helped migrant workers find work. The signs often advertised other benefits, such as housing, food, and schools.

SHARING WITH OTHERS

Paragould, Arkansas, now a busy city of about 30,000 people, was a small town of 6,000 or so when Emma Jean was growing up there. Two railroads, one controlled by J. W. Paramore and one controlled by Jay Gould, crossed in what would become the town of Paragould, named by combining the names of the two railroad **magnates** behind the town's birth. Emma Jean's family lived not too far from one of these railroads, which meant the family got a lot of visitors.

During the Great Depression, it was very difficult if not impossible for some people to find a job, food, or shelter in the town where they lived. Many people were forced to look elsewhere. Many of these

Potatoes were a staple during the Great Depression. A migrant worker is shown here working in a potato field.

people took advantage of the extensive rail network that had been built in the 1800s to travel in search of work. But if they couldn't afford a train ticket, and most people in this situation couldn't, they might do what was called "riding the rails." This meant sneaking into an empty car of a freight train or sometimes even

FAST FACT

POTATOES ARE A STAPLE FOOD IN MANY COUNTRIES AND ARE A VALUABLE SOURCE OF MANY NUTRIENTS, INCLUDING CARBOHYDRATES, VITAMIN C, AND SOME B VITAMINS.

Jay Gould, for whom Paragould was in part named, was one of the wealthiest men of the late 19th century, but he was also unpopular because of his often unscrupulous business practices.

clinging to the top of one. It was a very dangerous thing to do, and illegal as well, but people were desperate. It was risky in other ways too. Unlike in cities, there were no soup kitchens in the freight cars.

People who rode the rails (or traveled on foot) looking for work hoped to find a friendly family like Emma Jean's wherever they stopped.

FAST FACT

RAILROAD COMPANIES WEREN'T TOLERANT OF THEIR NON-PAYING PASSENGERS. THE SOUTHERN PACIFIC RAILROAD BOASTED THAT IT THREW 683,000 PEOPLE OFF ITS TRAINS IN 1931.

These two men were kicked out of the boxcar they were riding in when the railroad management discovered them.

Emma Jean said, "They were people that were just going from house to house begging for work, for food. Mother would always feed them, no matter what we had or what was left. She would fix a plate, and they would sit down on the back porch and eat their food."

FAST FACT

AT THE HEIGHT OF THE GREAT DEPRESSION, 250,000 TEENAGERS WERE LIVING ON THE ROAD OR RIDING THE RAILS IN THE UNITED STATES.

When they could, these people would pay for that food in the only way they were able to. "If she had some work for them to do," Emma Jean recalled, "like bring up coal, fill up the coal buckets, or bring in wood or pull weeds or whatever there was to do, they would do it, and thank

Many people shared what they could with hungry strangers who asked for help during the Depression.

FARM CRISIS

Rural households could often grow some of their own food. This saved them from at least some of the hunger suffered by people living in the city. However, the Great Depression hit rural America very hard. The worldwide depression reduced the demand for farm products. Farm income plummeted by more than half. That, in turn, caused the failure of rural businesses that processed crops such as corn and cotton or those that supplied farmers with seed and other supplies.

Though the Great Depression hit famers hard, the agricultural sector was already in trouble when the stock market collapsed in 1929. During World War I (1914-1918), farmers had to produce more food to feed the troops. To do this, many borrowed money so they could buy more land and more equipment. But when the war ended, demand dropped. Because farmers were producing more food than consumers were buying, prices fell. After the war, the price of corn dropped from 70 cents a bushel to 10 cents a bushel. Hogs went from 9 cents per pound to 3 cents per pound. Sadly, many farmers discovered that it was cheaper to burn their corn for fuel than to take it to market.

When they couldn't make money from their crops, farmers couldn't pay their debts or the taxes on their land. Many farmers lost their homes and land. In just one year (1924) more than 2,500 farms were lost to **foreclosure**. So when the economy completely crashed during the Great Depression, it hit farmers while they were already down.

her, and then be on their way." She never knew for sure, but Emma Jean guessed that these people passed the word among themselves that "this lady will feed you."

She was probably right about their guests passing on the word that you were likely to get a meal if you stopped by their house. People who rode the rails had something called a code, a secret system of signs and symbols that let other travelers know where it was safe to sleep, where they were likely to get a meal, and what places to avoid, because they might not be welcomed. These signs were often written in chalk or charcoal on fence posts, sidewalks, and the sides of buildings. This was yet another way people helped each other get through these desperate times.

Whether or not their house was identified in the code, Emma Jean's family and their garden had a steady stream of visitors in those years. This kind of generosity was common during the Great

Those who could share with others did. However, signs like this one sometimes turned people away because they couldn't take care of the people they already had in the town.

Depression, and not just in rural areas. However, people in rural areas were more likely to have a garden that provided enough food to share, at least during the warm months.

HOW YOU SEE HISTORY

1. During the Great Depression, the United States was in many ways a very different place from what it is today. Can you think of how some of those differences may have made the crisis easier or harder to get through?
2. What do the jobs Emma Jean's mom found for the people who traveled through looking for work or food tell you about life during those times?
3. Can you imagine what it would be like to get by mostly on food from a backyard garden? What foods would you miss?

CHAPTER FOUR

MOVE OVER AND MAKE ROOM

Like other people who were children during the Great Depression, Lenore was too young to know what was going on with the economy. But she wasn't too young to notice that her family was crowded into a small apartment and kept squeezing together to make room for more people who had nowhere else to live. In an interview, she discussed what that experience was like for a child in those days.

"WE HAD NOTHING"

Children know what's going on around them, but they often don't know why things are the way they are. Often, they just assume that whatever is happening in their lives is the way things have always been. That was the case for Lenore, who grew up in Chicago, Illinois, during the Great Depression.

"The Depression **era** started when I was about four years old," Lenore said. "I didn't know anything about it then. Because I was a kid, I really didn't know I was living during a depression."

Perhaps one reason so many adults say that when they were children they didn't realize they were living through a crisis is that unlike adults, kids can't compare what it was like then

Scan this QR code to watch Lenore talk about how space was tight during the Great Depression.

with what it was like before the hard times began. And in the case of the Depression, they couldn't compare their lives with people who were doing just fine. That's because almost everyone was living through the same crisis at the same time.

"We had nothing, but all our neighbors had nothing," Lenore said.

UNEQUAL BURDENS

Although the Great Depression affected millions of Americans, it didn't affect everyone in the same way. People of color faced greater challenges than white Americans.

In many places, Black workers were the first to lose their jobs and the last to be hired again, if at all. Even when jobs were available, they were often limited to lower-paying work. **Segregation** and discrimination made it even harder for Black families to access housing, education, and relief programs.

The Great Depression affected Mexican American families especially hard. Many were pressured or forced to leave the United States, even if they were citizens. White Americans pressured Mexican Americans to leave to free up jobs, wrongly accusing them of stealing jobs from "real" Americans. This led to hostility as well as demands for their removal from the workplace. This argument of Mexican Americans taking jobs from "real" Americans is an argument that some people continue to this day.

Additionally, state and local laws, especially in California, barred non-citizens from public jobs, which made it difficult if not impossible for Mexican families to earn a living. Federal authorities also conducted raids and forced Mexican Americans, including children born in the United States, to leave in order to keep public welfare resources with white Americans. It was common for Mexican immigrants to be denied public benefits because they were blamed for the economic crisis.

All these actions against Mexican Americans are referred to as a "Decade of Betrayal." The actions separated families and resulted in

FAST FACT

IN 1932, BETWEEN 40 AND 50 PERCENT OF BLACK WORKERS IN CHICAGO WERE UNEMPLOYED.

long-lasting trauma, with some people carrying their passports and citizenship information everywhere with them to this day because of what happened during this time.

"WE WERE LUCKY"

Lenore's situation was vastly different from many of those around her. She said, "We were lucky because my father always had a job. Most of our neighbors didn't have a job."

Lenore's childhood memories about that are exactly right. In the first few decades of the 20th century, Chicago was a major manufacturing center and one of the world's most important steel districts. But during the Depression, the steel industry suffered more than other sectors of the economy. Many steel companies shut down temporarily or even went bankrupt.

But it wasn't just steel. The agriculture sector was in crisis, too, and Chicago was home to many companies that

FAST FACT

BY 1933, ONLY HALF THE PEOPLE IN CHICAGO WHO HAD WORKED IN MANUFACTURING IN 1927 STILL HAD JOBS IN THAT SECTOR.

Classrooms during the Great Depression were often overcrowded because there wasn't enough money to pay teachers.

made farm equipment. Chicago was also the center of the meat processing industry.

All this made the situation in Chicago particularly disastrous. During the Depression, unemployment in Chicago was much higher than in most other big cities.

For people of color, unemployment was even worse than for white people. This was true for people of color even if they didn't work in manufacturing or meat packing. And many people, Black or white, who did have jobs were paid less, or sometimes not at all. In February of 1933, the city of Chicago owed public school teachers eight-and-a-half months of back pay.

SHARING HOUSING

But joblessness isn't the first thing that comes to Lenore's mind when she thinks back on the Depression. What she remembers

During the Depression years, families crowded in together.

During the Depression, people often delayed getting married because they couldn't afford a family.

most vividly is how crowded it was in her family's apartment. "We always had very small apartments. And the funniest part of going through the Depression is when somebody in the family would get married, and they couldn't afford an apartment, they'd come and live with us. And we would just, wherever there was room, we would let them live with us."

Several families sharing a home, even a small home, was common during the Depression. Just like sharing food from backyard gardens, people often shared space with friends and neighbors in worse shape than they were in. Sometimes two or more families would share an apartment and split the rent. But in big cities like

Chicago, apartments were often quite small. Making room for another family meant squeezing in tight.

"I remember, especially, one time somebody got married, came to live with us, and I wound up sleeping on a folding bed in the kitchen, because that was the only place they had for me," Lenore said, laughing. "So that was [the] Depression days."

HOUSING CRISIS

Even people who could afford rent had trouble finding a place to live. Between 1930 and 1938, Chicago was in the midst of a housing crisis. Few housing units were being built, and old ones were falling apart. On top of that, tens of thousands of families moved to the city hoping to find work. Of course, there was almost no work to find. Eventually, however, relief finally came from the federal government.

People did what they could for housing during the Great Depression. For migrant families, that meant living in tents such as these.

RENT PARTIES

When there was no money to pay the rent, people got creative. They threw rent parties. The host of the party would provide food and entertainment and push the furniture aside to make room for dancing. Guests paid a small fee—perhaps a quarter—to come enjoy the party, which often lasted well into the night. If everything went according to plan, the host made enough profit to pay the rent. Next week, the party would likely be at someone else's place. It was a relatively easy way for people to help each other, without straining their own finances too much. And everyone had a good time.

With so many people struggling to pay the bills, rent parties were common. These parties were most common in Black communities, but sometimes white people had rent parties too. The Harlem neighborhood of New York City was famous for them. But other neighborhoods and cities, such as Chicago, also had rent parties. There might be a dozen parties on a single block in one night. To get people to come to *their* party, hosts made clever invitation cards. The poet Langston Hughes collected many of these invitations, and those are now a part of a collection of African American Arts and Letters at Yale University in Connecticut.

Poet Langston Hughes documented rent parties, and other parts of life, in New York during the early years of the 20th Century.

Because the parties took place in the living rooms of small apartments, there wasn't much room for musicians. But that turned out to be a good thing. It led to the development of a new kind of dance music, Harlem Stride, that relied on just the piano to create a swinging beat for people to dance to.

When President Franklin D. Roosevelt was **inaugurated** for the second time in 1937, he said that he saw how many people in the country were undernourished and didn't have proper clothing or housing. He worked hard to develop programs to address these

Because housing was so hard to come by during the Great Depression, people slept where they could. This man is sleeping on the New York City docks.

problems. All these programs together are known as the New Deal. Some of them, such as the United States Housing Authority, provided funds to help local governments build more low-cost houses and apartments. The Public Works Administration also built some low-cost housing. However, most of it was racially segregated at the time.

BROKEN FAMILIES

"We were happy kids. We didn't know we were in a depression," Lenore said. But the adults knew. Despite Lenore's good humor about sleeping in the kitchen, it was hard on families to not be able to afford a place of their own. Many couples waited to get married and start families, hoping that times would get better. During this period, the birth rate fell below the replacement level. That means

FAST FACT

IN 1940, 1.5 MILLION WOMEN WERE LIVING APART FROM THEIR HUSBANDS. IN ADDITION, MORE THAN 200,000 ABANDONED CHILDREN WANDERED THE STREETS.

more people died than were born. This was the first time in U.S. history that had happened.

Even while people were delaying marriage, fewer people were getting divorces. This wasn't because they were happier in their relationships, but because neither the husband nor the wife could afford another house or apartment. Also, people were unable to afford the legal fees associated with getting a divorce. They were forced to stay together whether or not they were happy.

For this reason, and many others, the Great Depression was not a good time for families across the United States.

HOW YOU SEE HISTORY

1. During the Depression, many families struggled with their relationships. Can you think of why it might be hard to have a happy family in such terrible economic times?
2. Many people postponed marriage and parenthood during the Depression. What are some reasons, other than lack of housing, why people might do that?
3. Lenore remembers sleeping on a folding bed in the kitchen. Have you ever slept in a strange place when your family had overnight guests? Can you imagine what it would be like to sleep that way all the time?

CHAPTER FIVE

KIDS AT WORK

During the Great Depression, many families had to make do with what was available to them. This meant that some families lived in unconventional places, and some kids also helped with the family business. In an interview with Neil, he described living with his parents in the back of the family drugstore during the early years of the Great Depression and pitching in to help with the family business. It was good experience for Neil, who would grow up to become a doctor.

ONE ROOM

The Great Depression posed many different challenges for individuals and families. People had to be creative and find ways to survive. Some grew vegetable gardens and fed hungry people when they passed through their neighborhoods. Some people made room in their already crowded homes for friends and family who didn't have a place to live. Others hit the roads looking for work.

But for many people, hard times meant focusing on their families and their neighborhoods. That's what it was like for Neil's family. "Our life was centered around my father's drugstore," he said.

Scan this QR code to watch Neil talk about working in his father's pharmacy during the Great Depression.

In the days before big box stores, local pharmacies and druggists like Neil's dad were an important part of the community.

"We lived, actually, in the back of the drugstore, in one room, maybe 300 square feet." How small is that? Imagine a two-car garage, and you'll have a rough idea of what 400 square feet (37 sq m) looks like. Now remove from that image the amount of space a small bedroom would take up. Now you can see what 300 square feet (28 sq m) is like.

> **FAST FACT**
>
> HISTORIANS ESTIMATE THAT 3 TO 4 MILLION PEOPLE OWNED THEIR OWN BUSINESSES IN 1935. MOST OF THESE WERE SMALL STORES, SMALL FARMS, OR SERVICE SHOPS, SUCH AS SHOE OR AUTO REPAIR.

That's a very small space for three people to live in. But Neil's family managed to make a home there for several years. They had everything they needed, he said, "a kitchen, one bathroom, and the store was in the front of the building."

GOOD EXPERIENCE

The family lived in the back of the pharmacy until Neil was five years old. "Then we moved into a house," he said. But even after the

CHILD LABOR

Child labor had been debated for decades before the Great Depression. Before the Great Depression, many kids worked long hours at dangerous jobs. They often worked in places such as textile mills, coal mines, and glass factories.

Trade unions and social activists worked hard to end, or at least reduce, child labor. And by the early 20th century, the situation had improved, but not enough. In 1916 and again in 1918, the U.S. Congress passed laws that restricted child labor. However, the Supreme Court declared both of those laws unconstitutional.

In 1924, Congress passed a constitutional amendment to end child labor. But that, too, was doomed to fail. Unfortunately, not enough states **ratified** the **amendment**, so it did not become a part of the U.S. Constitution. Though the public increasingly disapproved of child labor, it was surprisingly difficult to stop the practice.

It wasn't until the Great Depression that the situation really began to improve. Many of President Roosevelt's New Deal programs had provisions that prevented at least the worst forms of child labor. The National Recovery Act, a labor law passed in 1933, had codes that reduced child labor. Then in 1938, the Fair Labor Standards Act went even further and set the minimum age for work outside school hours at 14. During school hours, the minimum age was 16. For hazardous jobs, the minimum age was 18. This had the effect not only of protecting children from abusive and exploitive labor, but also of freeing up jobs for their parents.

Shown here is a group of child laborers.

Children often helped out at home and with their family's business if they owned one.

family no longer lived in the back room, they still spent most of their time in the pharmacy, Neil recalled.

"My mother worked in the store; my father was there seven days a week. He ate lunch behind the counter, basically never left from 8:30 in the

FAST FACT

THE FAIR LABOR STANDARDS ACT, PASSED IN 1938, IS STILL TODAY THE BASIS OF LABOR LAW IN THE UNITED STATES.

Many people protested against child labor in the early part of the 20th Century, but their efforts weren't successful until the New Deal.

> **FAST FACT**
>
> IN 1930, ACCORDING TO GOVERNMENT DATA, AROUND 750,000 CHILDREN UNDER AGE 15 WERE FORMALLY EMPLOYED.

morning until 10:00 at night those years," Neil explained.

Neil's parents weren't the only ones who worked in the family drugstore. Neil worked there too. "I worked from age six doing various ... things, sweeping the floor, emptying the trash, delivering orders, because we delivered prescriptions."

Cash was tight in those days, of course, but Neil did earn some money for his work. "We'd get tips ... anywhere from a nickel to fifteen cents, which was big money then," he said.

Neil grew up to be a doctor. Perhaps the experience of working hard in the pharmacy helped him reach that goal.

FAMILY BUSINESSES

In some ways, family businesses, like Neil's family's drugstore, have an advantage in hard times. Family business owners don't have to pay employees, or at least not as many, because the family, including kids like Neil, do the work. That means they can often keep their businesses afloat when other businesses might fail. Also, people are generally willing to work harder for their own businesses. Even the employees they do hire are often better workers. Working for an individual or family that you know can be more motivating than working for a faceless corporation.

During the Great Depression, when there were few jobs to be had, people would often respond by starting a small business of their own. Because most people had very little cash, and banks weren't loaning money, they came up with ideas that didn't require much investment. They might open a small grocery store in an abandoned storefront or in their homes. They would sell canned food or produce from their gardens. Others chopped and sold firewood. People who lived near a river or the ocean might sell fish or clams they'd caught. Starting a business during a major economic crisis is a risky move,

Many people sold fruits and vegetables on the street to make money during the Depression.

This retail chain of supermarkets got its start at the beginning of the Depression.

but some people thought it was worth the risk. Some felt they had no other options. And like Neil's family, these **entrepreneurs** worked very hard.

Some of these businesses were quite profitable, and even went on to become huge successes. George Jenkins started Publix supermarkets in 1930, at the beginning of the Depression. Publix is now a chain of more than a thousand stores. In 1935, O. D. and Ruth McKee developed a recipe for cream filled oatmeal cakes and began selling the treats for a nickel each. That business eventually became the Little Debbie Snack Cakes brand that is still very popular today.

But these wild success stories are rare. For many families during the Great Depression, things didn't go as well as they did for these people.

AN ECONOMY FOREVER CHANGED

The Great Depression changed the way Americans thought about work, money, and government. It showed how quickly the economy could collapse and how many people could be affected. To this day, people keep watch of the economy and compare it to this period in time. Will there be another depression? Will it be as bad or worse than the Great Depression? Even almost 100 years later, a cautious attitude toward debt, banking, and consumption has passed down through the generations and made Americans highly aware of further economic catastrophes. It's also influenced how we react to high unemployment rates, market instability, and inflation.

The aftermath of the Great Depression led to many programs and systems that are still in use today. Banks are more closely regulated and the money that people put into them better protected. In 1933, the Federal Deposit Insurance Corporation (FDIC) was created to protect bank deposits. In 1934, the U.S. Securities and Exchange Commission (SEC) was created to regulate stock markets. Today, the government must intervene during economic downturns through monetary and spending policies.

In 1935, the Social Security Act was established. This is one of the most important things to come out of the Great Depression. This law provides financial support for older Americans and created unemployment insurance to help people who lost their jobs by providing them a portion of their wages while they look for a new job.

After the worst years of the Depression, the economy slowly began to recover. When the United States entered World War II in 1941 after the attack on Pearl Harbor in Hawai'i, factory production increased, and millions of people found work supporting the war effort. This helped bring an end to the long period of economic struggle.

The changes made during and after the Great Depression continue to shape the economy to this day, influencing how the nation responds to economic challenges. But just as important are the lessons people learned during these years: resilience, responsibility, and the importance of helping one another in times of crisis.

HOW YOU SEE HISTORY

1. In what ways can the effects of the Great Depression still be felt by Americans today?
2. Why do you think it was so difficult to pass laws that reduced child labor?
3. Do you think Neil's experience of the Great Depression was similar to any of the other stories in this book?

TIMELINE

SOUP BONES AND CARDBOARD SHOES: GROWING UP IN THE GREAT DEPRESSION: TIMELINE OF THE GREAT DEPRESSION

1929: The U.S. stock market crashes.

1930: A rash of bank failures begins, making clear the seriousness of the crisis.

1931: The most well-documented Hooverville starts in Seattle.

SOME WERE HIT HARDER THAN OTHERS: TIMELINE OF THE GREAT DEPRESSION

1932: Franklin D. Roosevelt is elected President of the United States.

1933: President Roosevelt is inaugurated and immediately begins taking dramatic steps to address the crisis, including reassuring Americans through the fireside chats.

1935: The Works Progress Administration (WPA) is established, providing many desperately needed jobs.

KIDS AT WORK: TIMELINE OF THE GREAT DEPRESSION

1934: The U.S. Securities and Exchange Commission (SEC) is created to regulate stock markets.

1935: The Social Security Act is put into place, ensuring benefits such as unemployment insurance.

1938: The Fair Labor Standards Act establishes a minimum wage and maximum work hours, including for children.

1941: The United States declares war on Japan after the attack on Pearl Harbor and enters World War II.

GLOSSARY

amendment: A change, especially to a constitution or similar document.
bankruptcy: A legal declaration of the inability to pay one's bills.
crisis: A difficult and often unsafe situation that needs immediate attention.
culvert: A tunnel or channel under a road or sidewalk.
dignity: Self-respect; pride in oneself.
dole: Government benefits paid to the unemployed or other people in need.
entrepreneur: Someone who starts and operates a business, usually at some financial risk.
era: A period in history.
foreclosure: The legal process of taking away a home, business, or other property when the person who owes money on it can't make the payments.
inauguration: The formal gathering that begins a president's term in office.
magnate: A wealthy business person.
mural: A picture painted directly on a wall, often used to decorate public buildings.
New Deal: The programs initiated by President Franklin D. Roosevelt to ease the Depression and help suffering people.
protein: An essential nutrient, usually derived from meat, dairy, nuts, seeds, beans, or grains.
ratify: To give formal approval, as of a constitutional amendment.
retreat: A secluded place to go for rest or to think or plan.
sandlot ball: An informal ball game, usually baseball, played in a vacant lot or field.
segregation: Separated, as schools, neighborhoods, or public spaces, along racial or religious lines.
soap opera: A television drama that follows the lives of the same group of characters, originally broadcast on daytime radio.
thrift: Careful management of money or other resources.

FOR MORE INFORMATION

BOOKS

Favreau, Marc. *Crash: The Great Depression and the Fall and Rise of America*. New York, NY: Little Brown, 2024.

Freedman, Russell. *Children of the Great Depression*. New York, NY: Clarion, 2005.

Marriott, Emma. *Did Anything Good Come Out of the Great Depression?* New York, NY: Rosen, 2016.

Mullenbach, Cheryl. *The Great Depression for Kids*. Chicago, IL: Chicago Review Press, 2015.

Sandler, Martin W. *The Dust Bowl Through the Lens: How Photography Revealed and Helped Remedy a National Disaster*. New York, NY: Walker & Co., 2009.

WEBSITES

The Franklin Delano Roosevelt Presidential Library and Museum
fdrlibrary.org

Find out more information about the Great Depression and the New Deal.

The Great Depression Facts for Kids
historyforkids.org/the-great-depression/

Learn more about the Great Depression, from the stock market crash to World War II.

Library of Congress: Voices from the Dust Bowl
www.loc.gov/collections/todd-and-sonkin-migrant-workers-from-1940-to-1941/articles-and-essays/the-migrant-experience/

Explore the experiences of migrant workers during the Dust Bowl.

PBS Learning Media: The Great Depression
aptv.pbslearningmedia.org/resource/fd6ec9b2-c160-4073-a62c-4d5f5e1b6562/the-great-depression-crash-course-us-history-33/

Young Adult author John Green explains what caused the Great Depression and clears up some misunderstandings in the process.

Walker Evans exhibit at the Metropolitan Museum of Art
www.metmuseum.org/toah/hd/evan/hd_evan.htm

Photographer Walker Evans documented the daily life of ordinary Americans during the Great Depression. This site has details about his projects and many of his photographs.

INDEX

PHOTO CREDITS

Cover, pp. 7, 32, 36, 46 Everett Collection/Shutterstock; p. 9 American union bank/Wikimedia Commons; pp. 10, 16, 24, 45, 53 courtesy of the Library of Congress; pp. 11, 18, 21, 30, 33, 44 courtesy of the National Archives; p. 12 WPA Volunteers of America soup kitchen Washington DC 1936/Wikimedia Commons; p. 13 Herbert Hoover 1929-1933/Wikimedia Commons; pp. 14, 23 Everett Collection Historical/Alamy Photos; p. 15 Seattle Hooverville sign/Wikimedia Commons; p. 19 (top) melissamn/Shutterstock.com; p. 19 (bottom) History and Art Collection/Alamy Photos; p. 20 Camerique/Alamy Photos; p. 22 Dennis MacDonald/Shutterstock.com; p. 25 WPA workers building stairway at Golden Gardens, 1936/Wikimedia Commons; p. 26 ClassicStock/Alamy Photos; p. 29 FoveatedPhotos/Shutterstock.com; p. 31 Photo of Tom Collins with migrant mother/Wikimedia Commons; p. 34 Glasshouse Images/Alamy Photos; p. 35 FAY 2018/Alamy Photos; p. 38 Unemployed men during the Great Depression/Wikimedia Commons; p. 41 Overcrowded School Room in Fayetteville North Carolina - Great Depression Era/Wikimedia Commons; p. 42 Vintage_Space/Alamy Photos; p. 43 NB/IA/Alamy Photos; p. 49 History and Art Collection/Alamy Photos; p. 50 Alpha Stock/Alamy Photos; p. 51 Une cuisine des classes populaires lors de la grande dépression/Wikimedia Commons; p. 52 EMU history/Alamy Photos; p. 54 David Tonelson/Alamy Photos.

ABOUT THE AUTHOR

AVERY ELIZABETH HURT is an award-winning science journalist and children's author. In addition to writing books for kids about topics as varied as dinosaurs and the civil rights movement, she writes about science for websites such as Science News Explores and *National Geographic*. She also writes about science for *Discover* magazine and *New Scientist*.

Avery has always been nosy (that's a good trait for a writer). So when she was a kid, she loved hearing her grandparents and other older people talk about what it was like living through various times in history. It really made the past come alive.